alef-bet

In memory of
Florence and Milton Gessner

Thanks to Sandy Brawarsky, Henriette Goldstein, James Gordon, Marcia Kaunfer, Rabbi Daniel Levine, Dr. Joseph Lowin, and Ayal Vogul for their help with the Hebrew material.

A SPECIAL THANK YOU TO FAYE R. HOUSE, PHYSICAL THERAPIST, for her help, support, and criticism in the creation and drawing of Uri (see author's note). Any mistakes or oversights are mine.

Library of Congress Cataloging in Publication Data Edwards, Michelle. Alef-bet: a Hebrew alphabet book / by Michelle Edwards.   p.   cm. Summary: This Hebrew alphabet book features three siblings and their parents in their everyday family life at home. ISBN 0-688-09724-3. — ISBN 0-688-09725-1 (lib. bdg.) 1. Hebrew language—Alphabet—Juvenile literature. [1. Hebrew language—Alphabet. 2. Alphabet.] I. Title. PJ4589.E38   1992   [E]—dc20 91-31011 CIP AC

alef-bet

A HEBREW ALPHABET BOOK

by michelle edwards

Lothrop, Lee & Shepard Books   **New York**

A Note from the Author

Hebrew is a very, very old language. It was spoken in ancient Israel many thousands of years ago, and has been kept alive for centuries by Jews and scholars, mainly through prayer and the study of ancient holy books such as the Bible and the Talmud.

Modern Hebrew was the dream and the work of a man named Eliezer Ben-Yehuda. He made new words from the ancient words and gave Hebrew speakers a way to say modern words such as ice cream, bicycle, and airplane.

The family in this book speaks Hebrew. They may know English, French, Spanish, or other languages, too. They may live in Jerusalem, Tel Aviv, New York, or Amsterdam. Almost anywhere in the world, there are Israelis and others who speak Hebrew as their daily language.

Although they are fictional, these characters have become my friends. Hannah is the *ema,* the mom. Matan is the *abba,* the dad. Then comes Uri (age 9), the oldest; Gabi (age 5); and little Lev, the toddler (almost 2).

Hannah is a children's-book writer like me, and Matan owns an art-supply store. Uri goes to school and is quite a good artist. He uses a wheelchair because he was born with spina bifida and can't move his legs. Gabi likes polka dots, dancing, make-believe, dressing up, and goofing around with Uri when he lets her. Lev likes his tire sandbox, stroller rides, kicking his feet at the moon, and goofing around with Uri and Gabi when they let him.

Hannah, Matan, Uri, and Gabi all came to life during wartime, so Gabi ends her book with *shalom,* the Hebrew word for hello, good-bye, and peace. It is her wish and mine that you may read this book in Peace.

How to Use this Book

Each letter of the Hebrew alphabet appears in the upper left corner of the page or spread. Its transliteration into Roman letters appears beneath it.

The Hebrew words appear on the lower left, and their pronunciations are beneath them. Hebrew words are read from right to left, and the marks beneath and inside some of the letters are vowels. Although Hebrew is often written without vowels, I have kept them in for beginning readers. There are no capital letters in Hebrew, but I made the first letter of each word larger to help you identify it. The English translations of the words are in the lower right corner.

It might help you to think of Hebrew letters with their English sounds, but there are some sounds in Hebrew that we do not have in English. The list below gives the closest sounds we do have. Remember, though, that people speak all languages with different accents and dialects, so some Hebrew speakers may pronounce the letters and words in this book differently.

א	ALEF	takes the sound of its accompanying vowel	ל	LAMED	L as in Like
ב	BET	B as in Boy	מ	MEM	M as in Mouse
ג	GIMEL	G as in Goat	נ	NUN	N as in Nice
ד	DALET	D as in Dog	ס	SAMEKH	S as in Sun
ה	HAY	H as in Happy	ע	AYIN	takes the sound of its accompanying vowel
ו	VAV	V as in Voice	פ	PAY	P as in Papa
ז	ZAYIN	Z as in Zoo	צ	TZADEEK	TZ as in TZar
ח	HET	CH as in CHallah	ק	KOF	K as in Kangaroo
ט	TET	T as in Toy	ר	RESH	R as in Run
י	YOD	Y as in Yo-yo	שׁ	SHIN	SH as in SHip
כ	KAF	K as in Kangaroo	ת	TAV	T as in Toy

Israeli Sabras are used to hearing Hebrew spoken with an accent. So, if you get a chance to meet a Uri, a Gabi, or a Lev, don't be afraid of the new sounds and words. Smile, say "Shalom," and perhaps they will share their *tzatzooeem* with you.

אalef

אַמְבַּטְיָה
(ahm-BAHT-yah)

bathtub

ב_ bet

בָּרָק

(bah-RAHK)

lightning

גימל

gimel

גַּרְבַּיִם
(gar-BAH-yim)

socks

ד

dalet

דָּגִים

(dah-GEEM)

fish

ה

hay

הוֹרִים
(hoh-REEM)

parents

ו

vav

נֶרֶד

(VEH-red)

rose

ז

zayin

זָקָן

(zah-KAHN)

beard

het

חָתוּל

(chah-TOOL)

cat

kaf

כּוֹבַע

(KOH-vah)

hat

ל

lamed

לְבָנָה

(leh-vah-NAH)

moon

mem

מִפְלֶצֶת
(meh-FLEHT-zeht)

monster

נ

nun

נוֹצוֹת

(noh-TZOHT)

feathers

ס
samekh

סְתָו
(stahv)

autumn

tzadeek

צְ עַצוּעִים

(tzah-tzoo-EEM)

toys

ק

kof

קוֹפִים

(koh-FEEM)

monkeys

תav

תִּינוֹק

(TEE-nŏok)

baby

Juvenile 492.4 Edw

Edwards, Michelle.

Alef-bet

DATE DUE

MAR 29 1993	
JAN 07 1994	